WORTHING

A Pictorial History

Frontispiece overleaf
The Old Town Hall

WORTHING
A Pictorial History

by

D. ROBERT ELLERAY

Fellow of the Royal Society of Arts

PHILLIMORE

1977

Published by
PHILLIMORE & CO. LTD.
London and Chichester

Head Office: Shopwyke Hall,
Chichester, Sussex, England

© D. Robert Elleray, 1977

ISBN 0 85033 263 X

Printed in Great Britain by
UNWIN BROTHERS LIMITED
at the Gresham Press, Old Woking, Surrey

For my children
LUCY and JAMES

Q.   *What is Worthing?*

A.   *Worthing is a hansome and fashionable watering and sea-bathing place, frequented by those who prefer retirement and quiet to the hustle and dissipation of Brighton . . .*

From Pinnock's *History and Topography of Sussex* . . . 1820

ACKNOWLEDGMENTS

First my sincere thanks must go to Michael J. Coviello of the Worthing Archaeological Society for his expert preparation of the photographic material for my book, and also to Mrs. Natalie Coviello and Miss Esme Evans for typing the manuscript. I should also like to thank Miss Fiona Clark (Worthing Museum), Henfrey C. P. Smail, and A. M. Rowland for their help and advice on various matters connected with the text.

In addition to material from my own collection used in compiling the illustrations I must record my grateful thanks to the following for allowing me to reproduce photographs and prints in their possession: Miss I. Allen, Lady Bassett (Melbourne, Australia), Becket Newspapers Ltd., Bentalls (Worthing) Ltd., K. Bryant, K. J. Chamberlain, The Reverend N. Evans, W. Gibb, P. E. Hayden, M. C. Joly, Loader's Photocentre, Mrs. E. V. Longley, George B. Shaw, Henfrey C. P. Smail, K. N. Strange, T. E. Tilley, Walter Gardiner, The Reverend P. Walton, West Sussex County Library (Sussex Collection), Worthing Hospital and Worthing Museum.

CONTENTS

Introduction

Old Town Hall, Worthing, *c.* 1887 (*frontispiece*)

INTRODUCTION

I have two objectives in publishing this book; first to stimulate a wider interest in the history and buildings of Worthing, and second to make available a pictorial record of the town. Worthing has never had a strong tradition of interest in its history, the task of recording and preserving having largely depended on a few individuals such as the Snewins, Edward Sayers, and more recently Henfrey Smail. This situation however, does not reflect a lack of available material about Worthing, for in 1924 a Sussex Collection was formed in the Borough Library which subsequently became, and still remains, one of the major local collections in Sussex. Towards the end of the Second World War Henfrey Smail began writing the *Worthing Pageant Series* which were published by the Worthing Art Development Scheme formed by William H. Odell, and became the first serious attempt to bring the history of the town to the attention of the public. These excellent books however, were published in small editions and are now no longer available. In presenting this pictorial survey of the town, therefore, I am seeking to keep alive an interest in its local history until such time as Worthing receives the comprehensive account of its past that it surely merits.

The Development of the Resort

By 1750 the increasing patronage of nearby Brighton by Royalty together with the growing popularity of the seawater cure prescribed by Doctor Russell and others, began to influence adjacent areas in the county. Parties from Brighton began to explore the Sussex coast and the merits of the sheltered and sandy beaches of Worthing were discovered. Soon visitors were tempted to stay in the district and by 1760 there is evidence that people were occasionally seeking accommodation in local farmhouses. About this time a certain John Luther from London seems to have realised the potentialities of the fishing hamlet of Worthing and became the first 'speculator', building a large house capable of providing lodgings for visiting gentry. This house was purchased in 1789 by the Earl of Warwick, and thereafter called Warwick House, and may be considered to be the beginning of Worthing as a resort town, which soon took its place among the group of fashionable watering places on the south coast of England.

At this time Worthing and its parent village of Broadwater were still small and primitive settlements where little had happened for hundreds of years and the inhabitants derived their livelihood from agriculture and a limited mackerel fishery. Only one road existed, leading from Broadwater to the fishing hamlet on the coast, running past the west side of Broadwater Green down what is now South Farm Road (then Brooksteed Lane). After fording the Teville Stream this road divided, the west fork becoming a bridle path to West Tarring; the east fork skirted the Teville Common and then turned south past the site of the future Toll Gate (erected on the site of the present Lennox Hotel in 1808) and then left into what is now North Street, eventually bearing south again into 'Worthing Street', later called High Street. 'Worthing Street', containing the Manor House, was the centre of the fishing community, and at its south end was East Lane (Brighton Road), and another common, the Worthing Common, or Saltgrass, which owing to persistant erosion by the sea had largely vanished by the late 18th century. The land within the hamlet was divided into four areas: West Field (from High Street to Heene Lane); Home and Middle Fields (from High Street to Ham Lane); and East Field (from Ham Lane to Brooklands).

The presence of a spring and pond at the top of what is now South Street made this area a focal point in the hamlet, and a track leading north from it to the Teville Common later became Chapel Road, first named New London Road, which in time superseded High Street as the main north-south axis of the town. From this track, another, now Mill and Richmond Roads, led westwards to the village of Heene. A linking path between South Street and the south end of Heene Lane (now Heene Road), called Cross Lane, formed parallel to the coast and later became Montague Street.

1. Hubert Edmund Snewin, from a photograph taken in about 1900. Hubert and his father Edward played a leading part in the affairs of Worthing during the 19th century, and it is due to them that the local history of the town was recorded and source material collected and preserved.

An outstanding feature of early Worthing was its isolation from the principal roads of the area. The marshy land east of Broadwater and the frequent inundation of the east coastal approaches by the sea contributed to this isolation, and made the opening of the Turnpike Road northwards via Findon in 1804 a factor of great importance in the rapid development of the town during the first quarter of the 19th century. Once the facility of Warwick House had become available and visitors had begun to take advantage of it, the hamlet soon increased in size with the commencement of building in Montague Place, Bedford Row, the Steyne, Warwick Street and the east side of South Street. The Steyne, which was completed only on the west side, was in many ways suited to be the focal point of the town, but when in 1835, the Old Town Hall was erected at the top of South Street this area became and has remained the centre of Worthing. These modest beginnings received impetus, and the fashionable success of Worthing was confirmed by the first Royal visit in 1798, when, on the advice of George III's physicians, his daughter Princess Amelia arrived in Worthing, lodging for part of her stay at Bedford House. Worthing quickly exploited these favourable circumstances and set about providing the basic amenities which were expected in the resort and spa towns of the period: a theatre, an assembly rooms, a covered baths, circulating library, and in many cases a proprietary chapel. All these desirable features were acquired in some ten years of great activity, during which time, in 1803, an Act was passed giving the small hamlet of Worthing town status. This 'new town' had a population of some 2,500. The Theatre, which was built in 1807 by Thomas Trotter in Ann Street, was without doubt the most significant achievement of the new resort, and played a key role in attracting both famous actors and patrons during the height of Worthing's fashionable success from 1800 to 1830. Happily the opening of the Theatre coincided with a second Royal visit, for in 1807 the youthful Princess Charlotte, daughter of the Prince Regent, stayed at Warwick House, and her presence in the town was the occasion of a number of visits by her father to Worthing.

Towards the end of the 1820s, however, the prosperity of Worthing began to falter and in company with much of the country the first symptons of a period of economic depression began to appear. In about 1828 the building of Park Crescent was abandoned owing to lack of capital and the local government of the town found itself on the brink of bankruptcy, and the debts which were incurred at this time by the Commissioners remained unsettled for many years. With the advantage of hindsight we may look back at this critical period of Worthing's history and identify the main difficulty experienced as an uncertainty concerning the town's future development. A transition had to be accomplished from the late 18th century type of watering place patronised by a relatively small number of upper class visitors, to a holiday and residential seaside town. For Worthing this transition was protracted, and these difficult conditions further aggravated by increasing problems concerning the inadequate drainage of the town. Growth slowed almost to the point of stagnation, and even the arrival of the railway in 1845 did little to reverse the trend which continued for some 20 years. The period of decline had two important results: first the cessation of large-scale building allowed subsequent mid and late Victorian infilling to give the town its uneven architectural appearance. Second, Worthing emerged from the difficulties a radically different type of resort, one that offered 'quiet domestic joys' to the increasing number of genteel families which sought it out for holidays by the sea: Brighton and other resorts were left to provide the 'garish' enjoyments for those who desired them — Worthing no longer wished to compete, it had established its own characteristic attractions for visitors and become a 'very nice place' for the discerning. By 1850, a crisis was reached over the drainage of the town, the old Commissioners showing themselves unable to act decisively to deal with conditions which had become little short of disastrous. In 1852 however, the old regime changed and a more efficient Local Board of Health was appointed, and it was to the credit of this new body, that a much improved sewerage system was introduced together with an adequate waterworks designed by Robert Rawlingson, who later in 1862 was responsible for building Worthing's first Pier.

2. Edward Charles Cortis, chemist, pioneer photographer and cousin of the first Mayor of the Borough, was born in Worthing in 1837. Later he moved to Scotland where he carried out research into the utilisation of seaweed. His photographs are among the earliest taken of Worthing and some are included in this book.

Eventually however, as social conditions generally improved the number of visitors increased, and Worthing began to benefit from its great natural advantages, its sheltered position, good soil, and excellent climate. By the late 1850s the horticultural potentialities of the area were being exploited, and very soon the town developed a market gardening industry of considerable importance, and gained a wide reputation for the quality of its grapes, figs, cucumbers, flowers, and, later, tomatoes. The equable climate was also soon recognised as the main factor in recommending the area as ideal for convalescence, residential settlement and retirement. By 1870, residential development had begun in earnest and new areas of housing appeared, especially in the western parts, where the Gratwicke Estate was commenced, and also around the village of Heene, which for some 20 years until 1890 maintained a separate identity as the New Town of West Worthing with a Board of Commissioners empowered by a special Act passed in 1862. On the eastern side of the town there was a more limited growth, but the estate known as Seldenville was built and a People's Park (Homefield) laid out with an attractive lake supplied by the Teville Stream. These developments were accompanied by the provision of various new facilities including five new churches, a new hospital (1881), new Assembly Rooms (1883), two railway stations (West Worthing, 1889 and the Second Worthing Station, 1869), new Council Offices (1887), Heene Baths (1866), and a new Pier in 1889. By 1890 the population of Worthing was 14,500, and on September 3rd that year the town was granted Borough Status and amalgamated with West Worthing.

The importance of Incorporation cannot be over-estimated, it provided a fresh impetus to the development of the town, and from it were born the policies which shaped the community which we know today. Promotion of the town in the modern sense now began. The first Official Guides appeared and Worthing was enthusiastically styled 'The City of Health in the Land of Gardens'; the 'town of the vine and fig'; even the English Madeira!, but above all the town became 'Sunny Worthing' — an appropriate slogan which is still with us!

The new Borough, after experiencing an early disaster in 1893 when an outbreak of typhoid fever caused the death of nearly 200 people, grew steadily until the First World War. Following the end of the War, a period of extremely rapid growth began and the Council's intention of doubling the size of Worthing was all but achieved by the outbreak of the Second World War, the population having increased from 35,215 in 1921 to 67,375 in 1939. The increasing use of land for building however, conflicted with the requirements of the market gardens and by the 1920s development was often taking place at the expense of the town's traditional industry. At first the result was a displacement, the nurseries moving from the central areas to the outskirts of the town, but as the expansion of the town reached a climax in the period 1918-1938 many firms closed down or moved away. In 1902, a Worthing Extension Order resulted in the ancient villages of Broadwater and West Tarring being included in the Borough and the way was open to development north of the railway line, leading to a radical change in the rural appearance of the town. In 1929, the parishes of Durrington and Goring-by-Sea were added to the Borough and with the exception of some minor changes in 1933, Worthing had reached the limits of feasible expansion. In the same year the town Administration moved into a large Neo-Georgian Town Hall, erected at a cost of £175,000, from the winning design of the architect Charles Cowles-Voysey. On January 1st 1933, the introduction of an electric train service by the Southern Railway reinforced the sustained efforts to promote Worthing as an ideal place both to live in and to visit. The years 1933 to 1935 also saw the opening of a Municipal Airport at Shoreham in conjunction with Brighton and Hove, the erection of the Assembly Hall, and two large cinemas.

The preoccupation of the town with expansion between the wars, was accompanied by an increasing neglect of the older historical parts of Worthing, and a significant lack of policy concerned with preservation. Areas containing the characteristic buildings and streets of the old resort, such as High Street, Market and Ann Streets, and several others fell into neglect and often unsightly decay. This unfortunate state of affairs prepared the way for extensive demolitions in the period 1950 to 1970, including the Old Town Hall, the Ann Street Theatre and the Marine Hotel. The loss of the Old Town Hall especially destroyed the architectural focal point of Worthing and removed the town's most characteristic view on entering South Street from the sea front. Historic buildings in the outskirts of the town also suffered destruction at this time, two of them, Selden's

Cottage and Offington Hall being of considerable importance. As a result of these events, much of architectural interest in the town disappeared, and Worthing, in the company of many other places, missed the chance of incorporating the best of its old buildings into an imaginative reshaping of its future townscape. These considerations should make the preservation of what is left a matter of public concern; for something is left, and if J. B. Parry were able to make a second visit to the Coast of Sussex, he might still summarize the appearance of Worthing in the words he used in 1833 — 'Worthing is not a regularly built town, but by no means suffers in appearance from this circumstance; and in fact, we think it gains by it, as the visitor finds at many turns new objects which he would scarcely have expected'.

Worthing, November 1976.   D. Robert Elleray

3. In 1973 Worthing Museum acquired a set of important water-colour drawings of the Worthing area by John Nixon (1760-1818), and they provide some of the earliest recorded views of the town. Here is his view of the Old Sea House Inn from the south west in about 1785.

4. John Nixon's sketch of the old Teville Toll Gate, near the site of the present Lennox Hotel. To the north west can be seen the Cross Street Mill, (or Worthing Mill), and in the distance the spire of West Tarring Church and Highdown Mill.

5. Another view by Nixon showing the south end of South Street with the original Marine and Sea House Inns. Beyond may be seen the south end of Montague Place. Note the complete absence of any raised promenade to protect the town from the sea.

6. Worthing's success as a fashionable resort began in the summer of 1798 with the visit of Princess Amelia, the fifteenth and last child of George III. She resided for part of her stay at Bedford House which stood to the north of the Dome Cinema until 1940. Amelia's delicate health was considerably improved by her sea-bathing at Worthing, but she later became an invalid and died in 1810 aged 27.

7. In July 1807 Worthing was favoured by a second Royal visit, the eleven year old daughter of the Prince Regent and Caroline of Brunswick, Princess Charlotte, who stayed at Warwick House. The engraving is from a portrait painted by Sir Thomas Lawrence in 1817, the year of Charlotte's tragically early death at the age of twenty-one.

8. This engraving of Warwick House (right) and the Colonnade (south end of High Street) appeared in the first edition of John Evans' *Picture of Worthing* published in 1805. The house was named 'Warwick House' after George Greville, 2nd Earl of Warwick, who purchased it in 1789. It became an important lodging for fashionable visitors and many notable people stayed there. The house stood just north of Elm Road and was demolished in 1896.

9. South Street in about 1820, showing the South Street Fields on the west side. On the left, with its sign, is the old Nelson Inn, the first meeting place of the Town Commissioners in 1803.

10. Liverpool Terrace may claim to be Worthing's best piece of Regency Architecture. It was built during the years 1814-26, and designed by Henry Cotton. No. 10 at the north end has an elegant porte-cochere. Formerly the land in front of the Terrace was laid out as a Pleasure Garden which included 'a splendid gothic rural bower, a bowling green and archery ground'.

11. The old Rambler Inn was one of Worthing's traditional haunts for smugglers and stood half way down West Street on the east side, conveniently near the sea!

12. (*left*) Princess Augusta, sister of George IV spent most of the Winter of 1829-30 in Worthing, taking up residence at Trafalgar House, later renamed Augusta House. This house became the Stanhoe Hotel and was demolished in 1948.

13. (*below*) South Street in about 1855, before the development of the open fields on the west side. Near where the pump stands was the site of the old Whales Pond. The well for the pump was constructed in 1809.

Worthing.

14. (*right*) Her Majesty Marie Amelie, Consort of King Louis-Philippe of France stayed six weeks in Worthing in 1861. In addition to her large retinue of servants, 'Queen Amelia' was accompanied by her family, including her seven sons. The party occupied the whole of the Royal Sea House Hotel.

15. (*below*) Ambrose Place, so named after Ambrose Cartwright, one of the contractors responsible for the building of the terrace. The buildings were erected between 1810 and 1826 and form a charming group of small regency houses.

AMBROSE PLACE.   *Worthing.*   Eng. & Pub. by Newman & Co 48 Watling St London

CHAPEL OF EASE.

16. (*top left*) An old print of Park Crescent as originally planned by Amon Wilds, the well known Regency architect of Brighton. Erection of the Crescent ended abruptly in 1829 owing to the general financial difficulties of the period, leaving the western half of the Crescent the west gateway and other villas on the south and west sides unbuilt.

17. (*bottom left*) An early photograph of about 1860 showing a water cart being filled at the pump formerly situated near the Old Town Hall.

18. (*above*) A panoramic view of Worthing drawn by G. Atwick in about 1846. The sketch was made from the top of the Sea House Hotel and shows the South Street fields which belonged to the Shelley family until 1866, when the land was sold and developed.

19. (*left*) Dr. Frederick Dixon, F.G.S., son of the Reverend J. Dixon rector of Sullington helped to establish the Ann Street Dispensary in 1829. In addition to his valuable medical work in Worthing he was a distinguished geologist and wrote *The Geology of Sussex*, published posthumously the year after his death from cholera in 1849.

20. (*below*) An early photograph taken by Edward Charles Cortis in about 1857 of the new Worthing Dispensary in Chapel Road. The foundation stone was laid by Mrs. Ann Thwaytes of Charmandean in 1845. The Elizabethan style building was enlarged in 1869, and renamed the New Worthing Infirmary. It remained in use until the move was made to the present hospital site in Lyndhurst Road in 1881.

WORTHING COLLEGE.
VIEW TOWARDS THE SEA.

1. (above) The once highly recommended
Worthing College for Young Gentlemen
occupied a large house later known as Beach-
field in the Brighton Road where the
Aquarina was built in 1968. The School
claimed to have opened in 1783, and moved
to Brighton Road early in the 19th century,
remaining there until 1900. The house had
stylistic similarities to Beach House.

2. (right) John Tidey, schoolmaster, artist
and poet, established the Heene House
Academy for Young Gentlemen in Heene
Road in about 1820. His two sons, Alfred
and Henry both distinguished themselves as
artists and exhibited at the Royal Academy.

23. The Worthing Exhibition was a notable event in the cultural life of the town in the 19th century. It was organised by the Worthing Institution, and held in the Old Town Hall from August to October 1855. The items on view displayed an extraordinary variety and included valuable pictures and manuscripts, hunting trophies, telescopes, sharks teeth and stuffed animals.

24. The gothic style Christ Church National Schools were erected in Portland Road in 1860 at a cost of £3,500, raised mainly by the efforts of the first Vicar of Christ Church, the Reverend P. B. Power.

25. A class at the Davison School in about 1905. The School was erected in 1855 as a Memorial to William Davison M.A., who founded the Worthing Free Schools. The School was rebuilt on its original site in Chapel Road in 1927 and later removed to East Worthing in 1960.

26. The Steyne Hotel in 1849. Built in 1807 by George Parsons it became the town's Assembly Rooms and played an important part in the social life of the resort. In the 1860s the south front was altered, and together with Stafford's Marine Library and Rebecca House (on the left), was provided with Victorian style bay windows.

27. Montague Place from the sea in about 1850, showing Sumner House on the north side. This fine open space was altered in 1877 when a roller skating rink was erected on the east side with subsequent development in the south east corner. Recently the houses at the south west corner were demolished as a result of the sea front development by Marks & Spencer.

28. The first important project undertaken by the new Local Board of Health was the construction of a water works on the site of what is now the Corporation Depot north of Providence Terrace. It was designed in a Lombardic Gothic style by the civil engineer Robert Rawlinson and built under the direction of Charles Hide during the years 1853-57 at a cost of £30,000. The bricks used in the construction were made on the site from local clay. The main tower was 110 ft. high, surmounted by a belvedere beneath which was a tank with a capacity of 110,000 gallons.

29. The Old Town Hall in about 1880. Worthing's first Town Hall was opened in June 1835 and built on land given by Sir Timothy Shelley, father of the poet, and one of the town's first Commissioners. The cost of the building, £1,500, was raised by subscription, and there is evidence suggesting that the architect was Decimus Burton. For many years the Town Hall provided not only a Council Chamber but also served as a gaol, Sessional Court, exhibition hall and fire station. On the left can be seen the old premises of Patching & Jordan, and Chapel Road, which still consisted of private houses.

30. (*left*) The south front of Beach House in about 1938. This fine Regency building was designed by John Rebecca around 1820, and was the home of the Loder family from 1876 until 1911. In 1908 King Edward VII stayed at the house for several weeks. Later the house belonged to the American actor and playwright, Edward Knoblock, but in 1927 it was purchased by the Council, and subsequently has been threatened by demolition on several occasions, notably in 1948, when the Borough's intention to pull it down was reversed at a Public Inquiry. Since 1927, both the fine gardens and the elegant interior have been allowed to deteriorate, and now bear little resemblence to their original condition.

31. Humphreys Almshouses were built on the south side of Christ Church in 1858. The handsome flint cottages harmonised with the design of the church and their destruction in 1970 was an architectural loss to the town. On the extreme right is the Spiritualist Church, opened by Sir Arthur Conan Doyle in 1926.

Worthing Pier
(from the West)

32. In 1861-2 Worthing built an 'elegant Pier of iron, 960 feet long, for promenaders only . . .' It was designed by Robert Rawlinson and cost £6,500, raised in £1 shares, chiefly among the inhabitants of the town. It was a simple jetty 18 feet wide with a small toll house at the land end.

33. A panoramic view of Worthing from the sea in about 1870. This interesting print shows the detail of the sea end of the first Pier, and behind the old Water Works.

34. The opening of the reconstructed Pier on July 1st 1889. Worthing's second Pier was designed by James Mansergh and cost £12,000. The ceremony was performed by Viscount Hampden, Lord Lieutenant of Sussex, followed by a Public Luncheon at the New Assembly Rooms Bath Place. The same evening the Pier was illuminated by thousands of coloured lamps, and a grand vocal and instrumental concert was held in the South Pavilion.

35. The Pier in about 1890. The attractive kiosks (which survived until 1925) were constructed by Mr. Alfred Crouch in 1884, one functioning as a toll house, the other as a 'fancy repository' and post office.

36. The old West Worthing Commissioners Office in Rowlands Road, built in 1865. The building was vacated in 1890 when West Worthing became part of the Borough. For a time it later housed the Public Library and School of Art. It was demolished in 1974.

37. A print of G. A. Dean's newly completed Heene Terrace and West Worthing Hotel, dated 1866. For some 15 years the Terrace and Hotel formed a separate West Worthing sea front before it was reached by the westward development of Worthing.

38. The Heene Road Swimming Baths were built in 1866 as part of the West Worthing development and designed by G. A. Dean in an elaborate gothic style. A small water works was added on the north side of the Baths and provided emergency supplies during the typhoid outbreak in 1893. The Baths, which stood on the site of the present M.G.M. Assurance block, remained in use until 1968 and were demolished in 1973.

THE PARADE, LOOKING EAST

THE PARADE AND BAND STAND.

NUFACTURE

PHOTOS BY POULTON

39.   Two views of the sea front from a folding guide. The lower picture shows the original portable town Bandstand occupying the site where later the bird cage bandstand was erected in 1897.

40. The West Worthing Hotel formed part of the Heene Terrace development and was designed by G. A. Dean in 1865. Following the Incorporation of the Borough in 1890, the name was changed to the Burlington Hotel.

41. A view of about 1890 showing the bottom of South Street. On the left is the Royal Sea House Hotel, and to the right the Marine Hotel rebuilt in about 1824 and demolished in 1965.

42. The well-known photograph of the severe tidal flooding, or 'overflow of the sea', which occurred on January 1st 1877. Until adequate sea defences were provided towards the end of the 19th century, Worthing frequently suffered from tidal flooding and inundations reaching as far as the top of South Street were not uncommon. The picture was taken from the Royal Sea House Hotel.

43. A boat being used in South Street during one of Worthing's tidal floods.

1. Attack on Mr. G. Head's House and Shop. 2. The Townhall. 3. The Police Station. 4. The Mob Attacking the Salvation Army Barracks.

THE SALVATION ARMY RIOTS AT WORTHING, SUSSEX.

44. The advent of the Salvation Army in the 1880s led to the unrest and violence in Worthing as in other towns. A 'Skeleton Army' was formed to oppose the Salvationists, and on August 17th 1884 serious rioting occured in Bath Place and outside Montague Hall where Salvation Army meetings were held. By the 20th the the position became so dangerous that Thomas Wisden, the local magistrate, called in troops from Preston Barracks, and read the Riot Act outside the Old Town Hall. Following this incident the trouble began to subside and the Salvationists became accepted in Worthing.

Skeleton flag was lowered, and the leader held up his hands to enjoin silence. The order was strictly obeyed. The Salvationists were called on to show respect for the Church, but continued singing. No procession took place in the evening, the special constables being relieved from duty immediately after the breaking up of the Skeleton Army on the beach. The feeling against the Salvationists still continues as intense as ever, but their antagonists evidently intend to keep themselves within legal bounds in their opposition."

RIOTOUS PROCEEDINGS AT WORTHING

45. 'Riotous Proceedings at Worthing' — a realistic sketch which appeared at the time of the riots.

THE SKELETON IN THE CUPBOARD!

Mistress. "I THOUGHT I HEARD A MAN'S VOICE DOWN HERE, JANE. I DO TRUST, AFTER ALL I TOLD YOU ABOUT THE LAST COOK AND HER SALVATION ARMY FRIENDS, THAT YOU'VE NOT ADMITTED ANY——"

Cook. "OH LOR, MU'M! THAT YOU SHOULD EVER THINK THAT OF ME!—WHICH I CAN'T ABIDE THE SALVATIONISTS, MU'M—AND MY YOUNG MAN A 'SKELINTON,' AND AT THIS MINUTE AT WORTHINK A FIGHTIN' THE 'ORRID WRETCHES!'"

46. A *Punch* cartoon published during the Worthing riots, demonstrating the amount of public attention they attracted at the time.

47. Charter Day, September 3rd 1890. The animated scene outside the Old Town Hall during the celebration of the Incorporation of the Borough of Worthing.

48. The first Worthing Town Council in 1890. The first Mayor, Alderman Alfred Cortis, is seated in the centre of the group. Worthing's local government was first controlled by Commissioners in 1803. In 1852 a local Board of Health was appointed which continued until Incorporation took place in 1890.

TO THE INHABITANTS

OF THE

BOROUGH OF WORTHING.

The Sanitary Committee of the Town Council again urgently remind you of the absolute necessity of

BOILING

WATER AND MILK

TO BE USED FOR

DRINKING & DOMESTIC PURPOSES,

And to continue this precaution until further notice.

WATER SHOULD BE BOILED AT LEAST 15 MINUTES.

By Order of the Committee,

W. VERRALL,

Town Clerk.

Town Council Offices,
Worthing, 18th July, 1893.

KIRSHAW, PRINTER, WORTHING.

49. (*right*) A Notice published at the time of the outbreak of typhoid fever in the summer of 1893. During the epidemic 1315 people caught the disease of whom 188 died. The epidemic proved a serious setback to the prosperity of Worthing.

50. The junction of Clifton and Richmond roads in about 1890, showing part of the West Gateway of Park Crescent. The Gateway was saved from demolition in 1958, and later restored to its original condition at a cost of £2,000, raised mainly by the efforts of Leslie Godden, Clifford Musgrave and Anthony Dale.

51. Disaster struck Worthing Pier at Easter 1913. On the night of March 22nd a severe storm lashed the south coast and in a few hours reduced the promenade section of the Pier to a twisted wreck.

52. The South Pavilion of the wrecked Pier was soon nicknamed 'Easter Island', and became a tourist attraction during the summer of 1913!

53. The re-opening of the Pier on May 29th 1914 was carried out with considerable pomp by the Lord Mayor of London, Sir T. Vansittart Bowater. The picture shows the arrival of the Lord Mayor's coach at the Pier.

54. A spectacular display by the Worthing Fire Brigade during the re-opening celebrations of the Pier in 1914.

55. Worthing beach and promenade to the east of the Pier in 1885, showing Rebecca House (named after the architect), the Steyne Hotel, and on the right York Terrace, later Warnes Hotel.

56. During the severe gale of November 11th 1891, two ships the German iron barque *Capella*, and a Norwegian schooner *King Carl XV*, were driven ashore at Worthing. The picture shows the stranded schooner which later broke up. The *Capella* was successfully refloated.

57. Free oranges were to be had on Worthing beach in March 1901. The fruit came from the wreck of the *Indiana*, and the incident was followed by a surfeit of marmalade in the town!

58.   The *Sea Breeze* was built on the Clyde as the *Adela* in 1877, and had a displacement of 206 tons, 13 tons heavier than the *Worthing Belle*. In 1897 she was sold to a French company and renamed *La Corse*. The *Sea Breeze* was a frequent caller at Worthing Pier after 1889 when regular services began following the construction of a landing stage at the pier head.

59.   The *Worthing Belle* was built on the Clyde by Barclay Curle & Co. in 1885, and until 1901 was called the *Diana Vernon*. Commanded by Captain J. Trenance she competed successfully in the Channel with the Campbell steamers until 1913, when she was sold to Turkey, and renamed the *Touzla*. After service in the Turkish Navy in the Dardanels she was broken up in 1936.

60. The Worthing Lifeboat *Henry Harris*, and crew in 1890. Behind (centre) is the old Lifeboat House, the small lookout turret of which still exists. The town's last lifeboat, the *Richard Coleman*, was removed in May 1950.

61. The Worthing Lifeboat Committee in 1902. Seated second from the left is Harry Hargood, O.B.E., J.P., who as Chairman devoted much of his time for some thirty years to maintaining an efficient lifeboat service at Worthing.

62. Worthing's premier Hotel, the Royal Sea House, was gutted by fire on May 21st 1901. The building was designed by John Rebecca and replaced a much older inn. The hotel became 'Royal' following a visit by Queen Adalaide, widow of William IV in 1849. The Arcade now occupies the site.

63. The Women's Ward at Worthing Hospital in 1912. A new Infirmary was opened in Lyndhurst Road in 1881, and renamed Worthing Hospital in 1904.

64. For many years the 'Cross Street Cemetery' was a familiar sight near Worthing Railway Station. The graves were those of Thomas Moore (died 1845), owner of the nearby Cross Street Mill, and his family. The four graves remained until 1908, when they were removed to Broadwater Cemetery. On the left is part of the old Worthing Station.

65. Montague Street looking west in about 1900. The corner shop on the left was Henry Lea's (later Mansfield's) Music Warehouse.

66. (*above*) Polish bear men were a common sight in England until about 1914. The photograph shows a performing bear in London Street in 1897.

67. (*right*) Number 43 Warwick Street was the last house to survive as a private residence in the street. In 1913 it became Leal's Creamery and was later converted into a restaurant. Note the similarity in style to existing houses in Bedford Row.

68. An Edwardian promenade scene at the bottom of Bath Place. The small shelter in the photograph was one of several which until quite recently formed a pleasant and traditional part of Worthing's promenade. Unlike Brighton, where similar shelters have fortunately been preserved, those on Worthing front were demolished in the late 1960s.

69. South Street and the Old Town Hall in about 1906.

70. 'Worthing's White Elephant' was begun as part of a grandiose scheme in 1893 to erect an Hotel Metropole and pier at the south end of Grand Avenue. The half completed block languished for many years before completion as the Towers flats in 1923. It was renamed Dolphin Lodge in 1971.

71. Worthing Public Library and Museum in about 1912. The building was erected on the old Richmond House site and designed by Henry A. Crouch, A.R.I.B.A., much of the cost being born by Andrew Carnegie, Sir Robert Loder and Alfred Cortis. The success of the project was largely due to the energy and imagination of the Borough Librarian and Curator, Miss Marian Frost, who had been appointed in 1901. The Library opened in December 1908, and continued until 1975, when the new Worthing Library was built in Richmond Road.

72. The opening of the Sussex Room in the old Worthing Public Library on April 12th 1924 was attended by some notable Sussex writers of the period. In the photograph are: *standing* left to right, Marian Frost (Librarian); John Oxenham; Viscountess Wolsey; Wilfred Meynell; Hadrian Allcroft. *Seated* left to right, Mrs. Henry Dudeney; Alderman J. G. Denton J.P. (Mayor); Alderman Mrs. Chapman J.P. (Chairman of the Library and Museum Committee).

73. A familiar war-time scene — troops leaving Worthing Station for the front in 1914.

74. The unveiling of the Worthing War Memorial on April 11th 1921. The ceremony was performed by Field Marshall Sir William Robertson, in the presence of the Mayor and a crowd of some 7,000 people. Behind the crowd is the Worthing Tabernacle and part of the old Davison School.

75. Children playing on the sands near the Steyne in about 1914.

76. Goat carts for children were a common feature at holiday resorts until about 1920. Here is an elaborate Cinderella coach on the promenade near Montague Place.

77. A crowded scene on the Parade in 1922. The fine cast iron 'bird cage' bandstand was erected in 1897 and the shelter on the south side 10 years later.

78. The sea front and Dome Cinema in about 1925. The Dome was opened by Carl A. Seebold, a Swiss, at Easter 1910, and was called The Kursaal until 1915. At first the building provided a roller skating rink on the ground floor, with a small 'electric theatre' in the small hall above. In 1921 the rink was converted into a cinema, and a popular dance hall called Billy's established upstairs. Seebold also ran the New Theatre Royal, Bath Place for a time, and opened the Picturedrome and Rivoli cinemas.

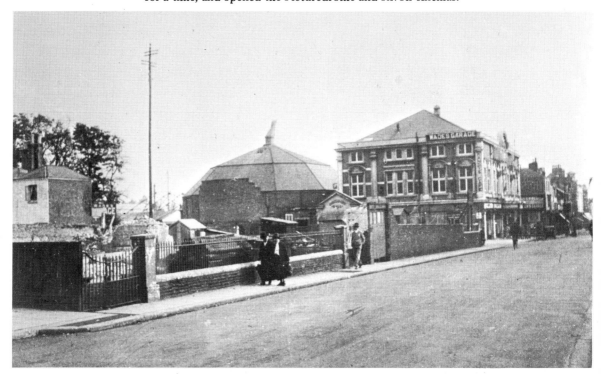

79. The site of the present Central Post Office after the demolition of Gloucester Lodge in 1928. Earlier the land was purchased by the Borough for a new Town Hall, but was later considered too small and sold to the Post Office who opened the present building in 1930. Beyond is the old Picturedrome Cinema, which later became the auditorium of the Connaught Theatre.

80. A Civic Reception outisde the Pier Pavilion for the Duke (later George VI) and Duchess of York in May 1928. The visit was in connection with an Appeal for the Prince Albert Convalescent Home, which once occupied part of what is now the Beach Hotel. The Mayor was Alderman W. T. Frost.

81. On May 22nd 1933 Prince George, later Duke of Kent, visited Worthing to open The New Town Hall. The photograph shows the reception at the Pier Pavilion. Standing to the right of the microphone is the late Duke of Norfolk who died in 1975.

82. A second disaster happened to the Pier, when on September 10th 1933, fire broke out in the South Pavilion, completely destroying it. The Pavilion was rebuilt in 1935, in a contemporary style designed by the Borough Architect C. H. Wallis, F.R.I.B.A.

83. The Pier Pavilion and Band Enclosure (later called the Lido) in about 1934. The two buildings were erected in 1925-26, following the purchase of the Pier by the town in 1921 and were designed by S. D. Adshead and Ramsey.

84. Bomb damage opposite the Town Hall in Chapel Road after an air raid on September 14th 1940. During the war Worthing experienced 1,028 alerts, and 268 bombs fell, killing 44 people and seriously injuring 72 others. In addition a total of 97 houses were destroyed by enemy action in the town.

85. The London—Worthing *Accommodation* stage coach. Before 1803 Worthing was virtually isolated from the main coach routes, Steyning being the nearest point where coaches were available. In 1803, the Findon Turnpike Road was opened and a summer service of three coaches a week to London began. The *Accommodation* coach office was in South Street (now Pressley's shop).

86. The Brighton to Arundel Stage Coach outside the Royal Sea House Hotel. James Town, wearing a topper, is on the extreme left.

87. James Town after several years as a postillion on the London to Worthing Coach, settled in Worthing in 1844 and became a successful job-master and horse bus proprietor.

88. A view of James Town's yard in Marine Mews, (now Library Place) showing two horse buses and a brake.

89. James Town's first omnibus outside the Chapel Road Dispensary. On the right is the rear of the Old Town Hall.

90. A youthful conductor in charge of one of James Town's horse omnibuses.

91. Mr. R. Stent was a successful proprietor of horse-drawn vehicles in Victorian Worthing. Here is his popular charabanc *Eclipse* in about 1895 outside the Royal Sea House Hotel.

92. One of Mr. Stent's advertisements.

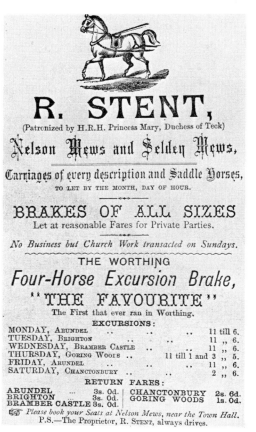

R. STENT,

(Patronized by H.R.H. Princess Mary, Duchess of Teck)

Nelson Mews and Selden Mews,

Carriages of every description and Saddle Horses,

TO LET BY THE MONTH, DAY OF HOUR.

BRAKES OF ALL SIZES

Let at reasonable Fares for Private Parties.

No Business but Church Work transacted on Sundays.

THE WORTHING

Four-Horse Excursion Brake,

"THE FAVOURITE"

The First that ever ran in Worthing.

EXCURSIONS:

MONDAY, ARUNDEL	.. .. ..	11 till 6.
TUESDAY, BRIGHTON	.. ..	11 ,, 6.
WEDNESDAY, BRAMBER CASTLE	.. ..	11 ,, 6.
THURSDAY, GORING WOODS ..	11 till 1 and 3 ,,	5.
FRIDAY, ARUNDEL	.. .. ..	11 ,, 6.
SATURDAY, CHANCTONBURY	.. ..	2 ,, 6.

RETURN FARES:

ARUNDEL	... 3s. 0d.	CHANCTONBURY	2s. 6d.
BRIGHTON	... 3s. 0d.	GORING WOODS	1s. 0d.
BRAMBER CASTLE	3s. 0d.		

☞ *Please book your Seats at Nelson Mews, near the Town Hall.*

P.S.—The Proprietor, R. STENT, always drives.

93. In 1897 one of the first hotel garages in England was built at the rear of Warnes Hotel. The picture shows the striking relief decoration over the old garage entrance in York Road, which was demolished in 1947. It depicted a 1902 Daimler, and the initials of the Automobile Club of Great Britian and Ireland, the predecessor of the R.A.C.

94. Early coaches of the Worthing Motor Services Company in Library Place ready to set out on local excursions.

95. An early motor bus outside the Old Town Hall. The Worthing Motor Omnibus Company was formed in 1904 in competition with the horse bus proprietors.

96. An interesting event in the history of Worthing's public transport was the introduction of a 'Tramocar' service in 1924 by W. R. Gates, a New Zealander. The open-sided Shelvoke and Drewry vehicles were small single deck buses with solid wheels, tiller steering and low steps. Later models had pneumatic tyres and were enclosed. At first only two buses were used on a 'Waterfront Service' between Splash Point and Grand Avenue, but by 1938, when the fleet was taken over by Southdown, there were fifteen vehicles operating a number of routes in the town.

97. The railway reached Worthing from Shoreham in 1845, and the first trains began running on November 24th. The original Station is on the right, while on the left is the second Station built in 1869. During 1908-11 the second Station was largely rebuilt and became the one in use today. On the extreme left is the old Cross Street Windmill, which was moved to a new site near Seamill Park Crescent in 1877.

98. A view of the second Worthing Station looking east in 1882. The gabled canopies over the platforms were an unusual feature, and three bays still (1976) survive at the west end of the down side.

99. The 0-4-2 Stroudley D-Tank locomotive No. 355, named *Worthing*, was built in 1886 and remained in use until September 1946.

100. Mr. A. T. Chapman, Worthing Station Master from 1883 until 1902.

101. Worthing Station looking east in about 1920. The locomotive is a re-built Billinton 4-4-0. Just to the left of the engine is the old Worthing Corn Exchange built by John Hampton in 1852, and demolished when the new Broadwater Bridge was constructed.

102. West Worthing Station was opened in 1889 as part of the new town of West Worthing. In 1905 a large goods yard was laid out on the west side and played an important part in the town's horti-cultural industry.

103.   The old and the new at West Worthing Station in 1933. A three-coach electric suburban set stands beside a 4-4-0 Drummond T9 locomotive. Electric train services between West Worthing and Brighton began on 1st January 1933, and together with the electric service to London, played an important role in the publicity to attract visitors and residential settlement in the town.

104.   Interested spectators surrounding an early aircraft on Worthing beach in January 1913. The pilot, a Mr. Simmons, had flown over from the Shoreham Aviation School to visit friends at Warnes Hotel, and the event was recorded by a local photographer, Otto Brown.

105.   Trips from Worthing beach by seaplane. From a photograph taken by Mr. George Shaw.

106. An advertisement post card issued by Smith & Strange in about 1912. The shop was one of the oldest and most successful family concerns in Worthing, founded by James Heather Smith in 1787. In 1906, George Neville Strange became a partner, and later the shop moved from the site shown here (now W. H. Smith's) to the east side of South Street. In 1919 the Brighton firm of Dawkins Ltd. took over, and in turn sold out to the Hide Group in 1946. The shop continued under its old name until it closed down in 1972.

107. Staff and delivery vans of the old Worthing grocers Potter, Bailey & Co. outside the firm's head-quarters at the corner of High Street and Ann Street. William Potter, the founder, was born in Crawley and apprenticed to Lintott's of Horsham. He opened a shop in Worthing in 1837, and continued in business until his death in 1896. The firm closed down in 1963.

LOST, FOR A LONG TIME PAST,
In Clouds of Dust,
THE WATER CARTS
OF THE TOWN OF WORTHING.

WHOEVER will find them, and set them to work for the comfort and convenience of the Inhabitants, will be liberally Rewarded:---

NOT by the Local Board of Health;
But by the Tradesmen especially.

Worthing, 20th April, 1855.

Royal Sea House Hotel Worthing

JOHN FOWLER,

Respectfully informs the NOBILITY and GENTRY who honour WORTHING with their presence, that they can be entertained at the above HOTEL, with every attention to their comfort and convenience.

FAMILIES may be accommodated with any number of Rooms, on moderate Terms.

COMMERCIAL GENTLEMEN also will meet with the greatest attention in the above Establishment.

J. F. has always in his Cellars a Stock of first-rate WINES and SPIRITS, BOTTLED ALES and STOUT.

FAMILIES provided with DINNERS from the HOTEL at their own Residences.

108. (*above*) A nicely worded admonition for the Local Board issued by the Worthing tradesmen in 1855!

109. (*left*) An advertisement published in 1850 by John Fowler, manager of the Royal Sea House Hotel.

110. William Walter founded the firm of Walter Brothers in 1846. He came from Marden in Kent.

111. Mr. Walter established his first shop in Montague Street and its success led to a second being opened in South Street in 1873. This shop, pictured below, continued until 1958, when the site was sold and redeveloped.

112.   The New Street Brewery in 1894. George Pacy's firm was one of the oldest in Worthing, and provided with water from its own well.

113.   Chapman's Tower Brewery in 1897. Much of the building remains in Warwick Road adjoining the Egremont Hotel. The Brewery's 'Family Pale Ale' became very popular and was described by a Brighton analyst as 'a high-class ale, pure and thoroughly fermented, of good flavour and stability, results only to be obtained by the use of the finest malt and hops, in conjunction with a good water supply.' In 1897 a nine gallon cask of the ale cost 9/- (45p).

114. A group of local market gardeners at work in about 1898.

115. An early Bentalls delivery van. Bentalls celebrated a century of trading in Worthing in 1975. The firm was founded by Frank Bentall at Kingston-upon-Thames in 1869, and six years later the present shop in South Street, Worthing was opened.

116. The Worthing cabbies assembled on the steps of the Old Town Hall in about 1890. For many years regular services were held for the town's cab drivers at Christ Church.

117. Christmas turkeys on display at F. Stubbs' shop in Montague Street in about 1892.

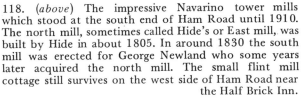

118. (*above*) The impressive Navarino tower mills which stood at the south end of Ham Road until 1910. The north mill, sometimes called Hide's or East mill, was built by Hide in about 1805. In around 1830 the south mill was erected for George Newland who some years later acquired the north mill. The small flint mill cottage still survives on the west side of Ham Road near the Half Brick Inn.

119. (*right*) A view of Heene post mill in about 1900. The mill stood a little to the south of Mill Road just west of Grand Avenue and occupied one of the oldest mill sites in the Worthing area—a 'Heind mille', being indicated on Palmer and Covert's Amada Map of the Sussex coast dated 1587.

120. The Worthing Division of the West Sussex Constabulary in 1892. The local force was amalgamated with the County in 1857, and until 1922 the Police Station was situated at the west end of Ann Street. From 1922 Thurloe House at the corner of High Street and Union Place (since demolished) served as a Station until the present one was built in 1939-40.

121. Worthing postmen outside the town's Post Office when it was situated on the west side of Chapel Road in 1883. Worthing's first Post Office was opened at the Marine Library (west of the Steyne Hotel) in 1798, and moved to Colonnade House in 1806. Over the years Worthing Post Office has occupied eight different sites.

122. Worthing Firemen assembled outside Warwick House in about 1895. A regular local brigade was formed in 1855, and became the Worthing Volunteer Brigade in 1869. Following the Incorporation of 1890, a Borough Fire Brigade was created in 1893.

123. Members of the old Worthing Volunteer Fire Brigade outside the East Worthing Station at the south end of Selden Road.

124. The old Worthing Fire Station was built in 1904, and designed by the Borough Engineer, Frank Roberts. It stood on the east side of High Street and was in use until 1961 when it was demolished to make way for Crown House.

Theatre at Worthing Sussex   23 Aug 1808

125. A sketch of the Ann Street Theatre as originally built in 1807. In about 1820 the front was altered to provide a more convenient porte-cochere. The Theatre stood at the south west corner of the present multi-storey car-park.

126. A photograph of the Theatre Royal in about 1958. The opening of the Ann Street Theatre by Thomas Trotter on July 7th 1807, was perhaps the most significant event in the development of Worthing as a fashionable resort. During the period 1807-1855 many of the famous actors of the time performed there, including Edmond Kean, and Mrs. Henry Siddons, who appeared as Portia in the theatre's first play, the *Merchant of Venice*. The theatre was demolished in 1970, after use as Potter-Bailey's grocery store for many years. Just to the left of the theatre is the first Worthing Dispensary opened in 1829.

Under the distinguished patronage of

THE EARL AND COUNTESS OF
MOUNTCHARLES.

THEATRE ROYAL, WORTHING.

On THURSDAY Evening, AUGUST the 23rd, 1832,

The Entertainments will commence with the laughable one Act piece of

JOHN JONES

Guy Goodluck, Esq...Mr. STANLEY.
Mr. Melton,........................Mr. COOK.   John Jones, (alias H. Smith)...........Mr. COURTNEY.
Cox, (Sheriff's Officer for Surrey)...............Mr. SEYMOUR.   Tapper, (for Middlesex)................Mr. WARDELL.
Eliza Melton,..............................Miss DE BURGH.   Jenny,........................Mrs. COOKE.

"ARE YOU ANGRY MOTHER?"
(ARRANGED AS A GLEE)

By the Misses Stanley.

AFTER WHICH, (COMPRESSED INTO TWO ACTS) THE OPERA OF

ROB ROY;

OR, AULD LANG SYNE.

Rob Roy,............................Mr. COURTNEY.   Rashleigh Osbaldistone,...............Mr. OLLIER.
Francis Osbaldistone,.....................................Mr. EDMUNDS, in which he will introduce the favorite Song
"IT IS NOT ON THE BATTLE FIELD."
Baillie Nicol Jarvie,....................Mr. STANLEY.   Dougal,...............................Mr. SEYMOUR.
Captain Thornton,........Mr. CORRIE.   Major Galbraith,.........Mr. REYNOLDSON.
Owen,...............Mr. JONES.   Mc. Stuart,.........Mr. WARDELL.
Sir Frederick Vernon,....................Mr. HEATHCOTE.   Saunders,...............................Mr. ROBERTS.
Helen Macgregor Campbell,.................................Mrs. STANLEY.
Diana Vernon,.....................Miss DE BURGH.   Mattie,.............................Miss STANLEY.
Jean Mc. Alpine,.................Mrs. COOKE.   Martha,.........Miss E. STANLEY.
During the Opera, a HIGHLAND DANCE, by Miss E. and F. STANLEY.

A COMIC ARIA by Mr. REYNOLDSON.

To conclude with the Musical Farce of The

BEE HIVE;

Or, Industry must Prosper.

Captain Merton,......................Mr. COURTNEY.   Hannibal Rattan,...............Mr. OLLIER.
Mingle,.............Mr. STANLEY, with the Comic Songs of
"SOME SAY WHAT CAN A MAN DO," AND "WHEN A MAN WEDS HE MUST
MAKE UP HIS MIND."
Joe,......................................Mr. CORRIE.
Phœbe,...............................Mrs. PETTINGAL.   Emily,.........Miss DE BURGH.
Mrs. Mingle,....................................Mrs. COOKE.

THE FOLLOWING POPULAR PIECES ARE IN PREPARATION.

"Olympic Revels." "The Invincibles." "Billy Taylor." and "Mary Stuart; or, the Castle of
Lochleven," dramatized from Sir Walter Scott's Novel of "The Abbot."

W. Verrall, Printer, (opposite the Theatre) Ann Street, Worthing.

127.   A playbill of the Theatre Royal, Ann Street dated August 22nd 1822,
produced by the local printer William Verrall.

128. (*above*) When Thomas Trotter built the Ann Street Theatre in 1807 he added the delightful Omega Cottage on the east side, as his own residence. In 1855 the cottage was acquired by Mr. Snewin and was finally demolished in 1970. Happily the fine circular bookshelves from its library were saved and reconstructed as part of the new Costume Gallery at Worthing Museum in 1976.

129. (*over*) The New Theatre Royal opened in 1897 on the west side of Bath Place (now Woolworths), and was converted from the former New Assembly Rooms. The theatre was launched by F. E. Ovenden, and later run for a time by Carl A. Seebold. It closed down in 1929, mainly due to competition from the cinemas.

130. (*right*) A photograph of W. Simson Fraser and Charles W. Bell taken in 1935. In 1931 Fraser and Bell formed the Worthing Repertory Company, using the Connaught Hall which was situated on the first floor of Connaught Buildings at the corner of Chapel Road and Union Place. The Company's success led to the conversion of the adjoining Picturedrome Cinema, which opened as the New Connaught Theatre in September 1935.

131. (*below*) The Pier Band in 1895. The group was formed when the South Pavilion was opened in 1889.

132. (*above*) Beginning in 1908, the St. James's Hall in Montague Street, provided the town with musical entertainment of a high standard. The picture shows the Mansfield Trio which was the resident ensemble. The musicians are from left to right, Winwood Mansfield, Herbert Moore (piano), and Charles Mansfield.

133. (*left*) Worthing's Municipal Orchestra began in the new Pier Pavilion in 1926 with an octet led by Joseph Shadwick. Herbert Lodge, pictured here, formed a larger orchestra and choir in 1935, and led it with notable success until his retirement in 1954.

134. The crowded Pier and promenade during an early Worthing Regatta.

135. A local cricket team, possibly from Findon photographed in about 1885.

136. A cricket match on Broadwater Green in 1837 between Sussex and an All England side. The green is of the traditional pitches of Sussex, and in 1805 a memorable contest took place there between the Lon Gentlemen, and Gentlemen from Worthing, Brighton and Shoreham for a prize of 500 guineas a side. local Gentlemen lost!

GENTLEMEN
AGAINST
PLAYERS.
A MATCH OF.
CRICKET
WILL TAKE PLACE
On BROADWATER GREEN,

On Wednesday,

JULY 18th,

BETWEEN
THE GENTLEMEN AND PLAYERS OF WORTHING.

GENTLEMEN.	PLAYERS.
Lord H. Paget,	Messrs. J. K. Jackson,
Lord A. Paget,	„ G. Cortis,
Capt. Parry,	„ R. Blaker,
R. C. Daubuz, Esq.	„ - - Robinson,
H. Warter, Esq.	„ O. Duke,
W. Blake, Esq.	„ H. Carter,
H. Cole, Esq.	„ R. Grey,
J. Davey, Esq.	„ J. Fillery,
H. Cecil, Esq.	„ S. Comber,
B. Brown, Esq.	„ E. Goodyer,
F. Lewis, Esq.	„ F. Patten,
W. F. Tribe, Esq.	„ - - Randell.

The Wickets to be pitched at 10 o'Clock.
Every Accommodation will be provided on the Ground by the Public's obedient Servant,
EDWARD GOODYER, Maltster's Arms Inn.

Wilkins & Patching, Printers, Worthing.

137. A cricket poster of about 1860. The Broadwater Cricket Club was founded in 1771, and the Worthing Club formed at a meeting at the Steyne Hotel in 1855. A new ground, the Manor Sports Ground, came into use much later and was used for County matches from 1935 to 1964.

138.   The Worthing Football Club Team of 1906-7. The Club was founded as the Worthing Association Football Club in 1886, and changed to the W. F. C. in 1900.

139.   Roller skating rinks became very popular in the latter part of the 19th century, and in 1877 this one was established by Walter Paine and others in Montague Place on land now occupied by Timothy Whites etc. On the left can be seen Sumner House.

140. (*right*) The Reverend Edward King Elliott, M.A., Rector of Broadwater from 1853 to 1904. During his long incumbency the Rector exercised a significant influence on the development of the Church in Worthing. He subdivided the Parish of Broadwater into the new districts of Christ Church, St. George's, Holy Trinity and St. Paul's, and maintained control of the patronage of the new churches. His educational work in the town was also important.

141. (*left*) The Reverend William Davison M.A., was appointed Chaplain of the Chapel of Ease (St. Paul's) when it opened in 1812, and remained there until his death in 1852. His work as an educationalist was outstanding and it was due to his initiative that one of the first National Schools in England was opened in Worthing in 1813.

142. St. Paul's Church in about 1900. In about 1805 the need for a church was felt in Worthing, and in 1809 a special Act enabled a Chapel of Ease to Broadwater to be erected. Governed by Trustees the Chapel opened in 1812 and was run on a 'commercial' basis, the pews being bought and sold, often for considerable sums. In 1893 the Act was revoked and a separate Parish of St. Paul's was created.

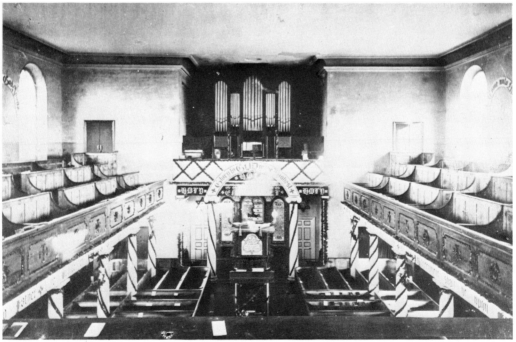

143. An early interior view of St. Paul's Church showing the old three decker pulpit obscuring the altar. Before 1893, when the present chancel was added, the altar was situated at the east end of the church where the font now stands. The remodelling of the interior at this time was carried out by R. S. Hyde.

144. Christ Church was the first 'Gothic Revival' church built in Worthing. The fine flint building designed by John Elliott of Chichester, was opened in 1843, and became a Parish Church in July 1855. The picture shows the Church before the choir vestry was added to the south east corner in 1893.

145. The Reverend Philip Bennett Power, M.A., first Vicar of Christ Church, was appointed when the Parish was formed in 1855, 12 years after the Church was opened. After an active and successful ministry at Christ Church Power left Worthing in 1864, devoting the rest of his life to preaching and writing, and became a prolific author of tracts and religious books.

146. The Roman Catholic Church in about 1910. Public worship by Roman Catholics in Worthing began in the Chapel at Offington Hall, owned by Thomas Gaisford. Later in 1864 the Church of St. Mary of the Angels together with the Convent of Our Lady of Sion was built in Crescent Road, designed in the French Gothic style by Henry Clutton.

147. St. George's East Worthing was built in 1868 from designs by George Trufitt. The site was given by the Rector of Broadwater and the building was the second of the new gothic style churches erected in Worthing in the 19th century.

148. The Church of St. Botolph's Heene in about 1890, before the enlargement of the south aisle and transept which was carried out in 1905. The Church, designed by Edmund E. Scott of Brighton, was erected in 1873 on the site of the old Heene Chapel which was partly demolished in 1766. Part of this Chapel survives as a small ruin to the east of the present Church.

149. The Heene bell ringers in about 1890. A peal of eight bells cast by John Warner & Sons was provided when the tower was added to the Church in 1880.

150. The tower and spire of Holy Trinity Church Shelley Road, nearing completion in 1887. The Church was designed by Coe and Robinson, and opened in 1883 to cater for the rapidly growing Gratwicke Estate in the western part of Christ Church Parish.

151. St. Andrews Church, Clifton Road, and its builders in 1886. St. Andrews, designed by Sir Arthur Blomfield, was Worthing's first 'High Church', and erected mainly with money given by George Wedd of Charmandean. Although completed in 1883 the building was not dedicated for use until 1888, owing to the bitter opposition of the Rector of Broadwater and the Vicar of Christ Church which led to an unsuccessful Appeal in the House of Lords to prevent its opening.

152. The old Congregational Chapel at the corner of Portland Road and Montague Street (now shops). In 1842 this Chapel replaced a smaller building which had been erected in 1804, and was the first non-conformist Chapel opened in Worthing. In 1903 the Congregation moved to the present Church in Shelley Road, and the old Chapel became the Winter Hall where silent films and other entertainment was given.

153. The Christian Literary Institute, Montague Street, was built by the Congregationalists next to their Chapel in 1862—'to promote Sunday and weekday instruction for the poor children, mechanics, and fishermen of the town and provide a useful library for the common folk'. The gothic front was demolished soon after this photograph was taken in the 1930s.

154. The old Methodist Chapel in Bedford Row, afterwards called the Bedford Hall, and used as an auction room. The Classical facade with Egyptian style windows was designed by Charles Hide in 1838. The Wesleyan Methodists had moved to Bedford Row from a small chapel in Marine Place, and later built the Steyne Gardens Church in 1901.

155. (*above*) St. James's Hall (also called Montague Hall and now Horne's Outfitters) was built in 1839 as the Worthing Tabernacle. It was subsequently used by various religious denominations, but in about 1860 it became a theatre and music hall. Later it again became the Worthing Tabernacle founded by the Reverend C. Douglas Crouch, and then Mansfields Music Warehouse, when the old chapel auditorium was used as a concert hall for several years.

156. (*right*) C. Douglas Crouch was born at Bromley in 1853 and became a Baptist Pastor, first at Shoreham then at Christ Church Road Baptist Church. Later he resigned and established the Worthing Tabernacle in St. James's Hall Montague Street, then moving to the present Worthing Tabernacle in Chapel Road which he opened in 1908.

157. An aquatint of Broadwater showing the tower of the Parish Church of St. Mary, the spire of which was removed in 1826. The church is Transitional Norman and contains two fine 16th century tombs of the De La Warrs of Offington Hall.

158. The restoration of the chancel of St. Mary's Broadwater in 1857 by Charles Hyde which saved the structure from collapse. The bulging sides were gradually corrected by successively heating and cooling iron braces passed through the walls, the operation being known at the time as 'Mr. Hyde's Experiment'.

159. (*above*) The old Rectory Barn which once stood on the west side of Broadwater Road, opposite the Church.

160. (*right*) Broadwater Fair, Easter 1891. The little boy had obviously been successful at the coconut shy!

161. Broadwater Street West in about 1885. On the right is the Maltsters' Arms kept by Mr. W. Pay from 1872 until 1889. For many years the Rector of Broadwater and others made efforts to have the inn closed, but without success!

162. Charmandean was built by John Penfold in about 1810, and stood near Longlands Glade. In 1842 the house was purchased by William Thwaytes, whose wife Ann enlarged it considerably and became known for her support of local causes including the Chapel Road Infirmary and the restoration of Broadwater Church. In 1871 George Wedd, benefactor of St. Andrews Church, Clifton Road, occupied the house. After being a school for several years the building was demolished in 1963.

163. Broadwater, or Ballard's Mill (also called Cissbury or Offington Mill) was a post mill worked by Charles Ballard from about 1839, and later by his son Richard. The mill belonged to Henry Isted from 1882 until 1901, when it ceased working. It stood near the present Mill Plantation on the southern slopes of Cissbury. The photograph shows the Mill in decay in about 1914.

164. Richard Jefferies was the son of a Wiltshire farmer and became a gifted nature writer. He moved to Goring in 1886, and died there at Sea View (now called Jefferies House) in August 1887. He is buried in Broadwater Cemetery.

165. (*above*) A harvest scene at West Tarring in about 1820 showing St. Andrews Church and the old Church Farm, where Thomas Henty lived before emigrating to Australia.

166. (*left*) Thomas Henty purchased Church Farm, West Tarring in 1796, where he farmed successfully and raised Merino sheep. Owing to the general depression in agriculture in the 1820s, Thomas decided to emigrate to Australia, and sailed from Littlehampton in June 1829 on a chartered vessel containing his family, employees and all his livestock and equipment. The arrival of the Henty family in Australia led to the successful development of sheep farming in that country.

167. A photograph of Parsonage Row Cattages in High Street, West Tarring, taken by John H. B. Fletcher in 1896. The Cottages are fine examples of 15th century timber framed building and since 1927 have been maintained as a small museum by the Sussex Archaeological Trust. In 1926 the Row was saved from demolition by the action of Mr. Mackenzie Ross of Ferring and the Royal Society of Arts' Fund for the Preservation of Ancient Cottages.

168. St. Andrew's West Tarring where John Selden was baptised in 1584. The Church is Early English—Perpendicular in style, and the tall steeple has long been a distinctive landmark in the area.

169. The Old Palace of the Archbishops of Canterbury at West Tarring from a photograph of about 1868. M. A. Lower described the Palace as 'among the most perfect specimens of ancient architecture in the Rape of Bramber'. The building dates from the period 1350-1450, and has a fine stone roof. It is said that Thomas a Becket occasionally stayed a the Palace.

170. Another view of the Palace from a late 18th century print.

171. Restoration work beginning in the ruins of the old Durrington Chapel in 1914. The original building had been wrecked by the Parliamentarians in the Civil War owing to the Royalist sympathies of the incumbant, William Stanley.

172. **The** Bishop of Chichester leaving the temporary Iron Chapel at Durrington to dedicate the new Church of St. Symphorian in October 1915. The church incorporates part of the original 14th century building. The present chancel was added in 1941.

173. A photograph by John H. B. Fletcher of Selden's Cottage at Salvington in 1895. The cottage, once part of of Lacies Farm was the birth place of John Selden, the famous jurist and historian in 1584. After 1930 the cottage fell into neglect and was demolished in 1956, robbing Worthing of one of its most historic buildings.

174. Offington Hall, a building of great antiquity and historic interest, was demolished in 1963. It was originally a manor held by Earl Godwin before the Conquest, and in the 13th century by Thomas de Offington. Later it belonged to the De La Warr family, and in 1747 was inherited by John Margesson who rebuilt much of the house in a Georgian style. In 1858, the Hall was bought by Thomas Gaisford who added a gothic wing on the west side which included a fine library and private chapel.

175. St. Mary's Church, Goring in 1804. In 1837 this building was demolished and the present gothic style church erected at the expense of David Lyon. The architect was Decimus Burton.

176. Harvest scene at Goring in about 1910. On the right is the spire of St. Mary's Church.

177. Field Place Sports and Social Centre in 1960. The house, which was purchased by the Borough in 1956, is one of the ancient manors of the area. It belonged to the Cooke family from about 1400 until 1726, when it passed to the Westbrooke-Richardsons, and later to Colonel E. W. Margesson. The interior still retains the 'Oak Room' which has richly carved Jacobean panelling, but the house was extensively altered in the late 18th century and the east front dates from about 1800. Around 1800 the house and farm were occupied by Samuel Henty, and Thomas Henty's letter enquiring about prospects in Australia was written from Field Place in 1822.

178. Goring Hall in about 1895. The present Goring Hall School was founded by A. G. N. Green, B.A., in 1938, and the building was a replica of an earlier one burned down in 1888. The tower has subsequently been removed. For many years the Hall was the seat of the Lyon family.

179. The Tomb with a view! The grave of John Olliver (1709-1793) on Highdown Hill. The 'Miller's Tomb' has been one of the sights of Worthing since the beginning of the 19th century. Olliver worked Highdown Mill which once stood near the summit and had a reputation for eccentricity and smuggling. Many years before his death he built his tomb and embellished it with his own verses. Later his wife established a tea chalet near the tomb which became popular with visitors to Worthing.

180. Courtlands much as it was originally built in 1820 by William Olliver. In 1902 the house was acquired by Paul Schweder who in a few years rebuilt the mansion, incorporating into it materials recovered from various important houses, such as Lebanon House, Twickenham (Robert Adam, 1762), the Cordwainers' Hall London, and the Ritz Hotel in Paris, The house was converted into a post operative recovery hospital in 1951 by Worthing Hospital, and in 1973 was occupied by the West Sussex Area Health Authority.

181. Castle Goring was begun in about 1790 by Sir Bysshe Shelley, grandfather of the Poet, and completed some twenty-five years later. The mansion is an interesting combination of Classical and Gothick styles, the Palladian south front (shown here) was designed by Biagio Rebecca, and the north side apparently inspired by portions of Arundel Castle. In 1845 the building, which had cost about £90,000 was sold by the Shelley's to Captain Pechell of Goring for £11,250.

SOME DATES IN WORTHING'S HISTORY

1584	John Selden, jurist and historian, born at Lacies Farm, Salvington.
c.1759	Warwick House built by John Luther.
1733	John Wilkes visited Worthing to watch the return of the mackerel fishing fleet.
1798	Visit of Princess Amelia, daughter of George III.
1803	Worthing Town Act passed. First Town Commissioners took office on 13 June.
1804	First Non-Conformist Chapel (later Congregational) built at the south end of Portland Road.
1805	John Evans published the town's first guide *Picture of Worthing*.
1807	Visit of Princess Charlotte, daughter of the Prince Regent.
1807	The Ann Street Theatre, built by Thomas Trotter, opened on 7 July.
1810	Town Market opened in Ann Street.
1812	The Chapel of Ease (now St. Paul's) opened.
1813	Worthing Free School for boys opened on 1 January.
1814	Liverpool Terrace begun.
1827	Sea House Hotel re-built.
c.1829	Park Crescent begun.
1829	Visit of Princess Augusta, sister of George IV.
1829	Worthing's first Dispensary opened in Ann Street.
1829	Thomas Henty emigrated to Australia.
1832	Smuggling affray in High Street.
1834	Gas Works opened in Anchor Lane (now Lyndhurst Road).
1835	Old Town Hall opened.
1838	Charles Hide's *Survey* and 25 in. Map of Worthing published.
1838	Worthing Institute founded.
1843	Christ Church opened.
1844	Second Worthing Dispensary (later Infirmary) built in Chapel Road.
1845	Railway opened between Worthing and Shoreham. Services began on 24 November.
1850	Publication of Edward Cresy's Report on the sanitary conditions of Worthing.
1850	Eleven local fishermen drowned attempting to assist the *Lalla Rookh* in distress off Worthing.
1851	Portable stocks outside Old Town Hall used for the last time.
1852	John Hampton built the Worthing Corn Exchange at Broadwater Bridge.
1852	Worthing Local Board of Health replaced Commissioners.
1852	Death of Rev. William Davison on 24 April.
1853	Great hailstorm severely damaged crops and property on 7 July.
1855	The Worthing Exhibition held at the Old Town Hall.
1855	Ann Street Theatre closed on 6 December.
1855	Davison Memorial School opened in Chapel Road.
1855	The Lancing road washed away by rough seas.
1857	Water Works completed.

1862	First Pier opened.
1862	The Christian Literary Insititution opened in Montague Street.
1864	The Roman Catholic Church of St. Mary of the Angels and Sion Convent opened.
1865	Commissioners appointed to administer the 'New Town' of West Worthing.
1865	Heene Terrace and Baths built as part of the new town of West Worthing.
1866	Worthing's first lifeboat, the *Jane*, launched.
1868	St. George's Church opened in East Worthing.
1870	First Worthing street directory published by Frederick Lucy.
1873	St. Botolph's Church, Heene, opened.
1877	1 January, severe sea flooding.
1881	Worthing Baptist Church begun in Christ Church Road.
1881	Worthing Hospital opened in Lyndhurst Road.
1883	Holy Trinity Church opened in Shelley Road.
1883	*Worthing Gazette* first published 12 July.
1884	Salvation Army riots.
1887	New Town Offices built in Liverpool Road.
1888	Goring Hall burned down.
1888	St. Andrews, Clifton Road, opened.
1889	West Worthing railway station opened.
1889	The reconstructed Pier with south Pavilion opened.
1890	September 3rd Charter Day — Worthing created a Borough and amalgamated with West Worthing.
1893	Chapel of Ease became the Parish Church of St. Pauls.
1893	Serious typhoid epidemic in Worthing from May to September.
1896	Warwick House demolished.
1896	Rafferty's map of Worthing published.
1897	New Theatre Royal, Bath Place , opened.
1899	St. Matthew's Church, Tarring Road, opened.
1901	Steyne Gardens Methodist Church opened.
1901	Public electricity supply began.
1901	Royal Sea House Hotel burned down.
1901	Portion of a Roman 'milestone' found in Grand Avenue.
1902	Borough enlarged to include Broadwater, and West Tarring.
1903	New Congregational Church, Shelley Road, opened.
1908	Public Library and Museum opened.
1911	Present railway station completed.
1913	Severe storm destroyed major part of the Pier.
1920	*Worthing Herald* first published 15 May.
1923	Worthing's first major cinema, the Rivoli, opened in Chapel Road.
1925	Band enclosure (now Lido) replaced the old birdcage bandstand.
1926	Pavilion Concert Hall built at landward end of Pier.
1929	Borough enlarged to include Durrington and Goring.
1931	Connaught Theatre opened 25 April.
1933	1 January electric train service began.
1933	Pier South Pavilion destroyed by fire.
1933	The new (present) Town Hall opened.
1933	Plaza Cinema opened in Rowlands Road.
1934	Odeon Cinema opened by Earl Winterton.

1935	The Assembly Hall opened in Stoke Abbott Road.
1935	Pier re-opened.
1935	New Connaught Theatre, Union Place, opened on 25 September.
1936	Brighton Hove and Worthing Municipal Airport opened at Shoreham.
1948	Beach House saved from demolition.
1956	John Selden's cottage at Salvington demolished.
1956	Seaweed Report published by Council.
1963	Offington Hall and Charmandean demolished.
1969	New Broadwater Bridge opened.
1970	Old Theatre, Omega Cottage, the north side of Ann Street and Market Street demolished.
1972	The Warren demolished.
1974	Guildbourne Centre opened.

SELECT BIBLIOGRAPHY

EVANS, John, *Picture of Worthing* . . . (London and Worthing, 1805). 118pp., illus. A second edition, 2 Vols. (1814).

MACKCOULL, James, *A Sketch of Worthing and its environs* . . . (Worthing, J. Mackcoull, Apollo Library, 1813). 209pp., illus.

SHEARSMITH, John, *A topographical description of Worthing* . . . *to which is prefixed a concise essay on cold and warm bathing.* (Worthing, G. Verrall, 1824). 115pp., front.

WALLIS, E., *Wallis's Stranger in Worthing; or a new guide to that delightful watering place.* . . ([Worthing] E. Wallis, 1832). 65pp., maps.

CRESY, Edward, *Report* . . . *on a preliminary inquiry into the sewerage, drainage, and supply of water, and the sanitary condition of the inhabitants of* . . . *Worthing* (H.M.S.O., 1850). 36pp., tables.

WARTER, Reverend John Wood, *Appendicia et pertinentiae: or, Parochial Fragments relating to the Parish of West Tarring.* . . (Francis and John Rivington, 1853). 369pp.

WARTER, Reverend John Wood, *The Sea-board and the Down; or, My Parish in the South* [West Tarring] . . . 2 Vols. (Rivingtons, 1860).

BARKER, Walter G., *On the Climate of Worthing.* . . 2nd ed. (John Churchill, 1867). 116pp., front.

FENTON, James A., 'Worthing 200 years ago' in *Sussex Archaeological Collections*, Vol. 35 (1887), pp., 93-100.

KELLY, Dr. Charles, *Report on the Enteric Fever in 1893 in the Borough of Worthing, Broadwater and West Tarring* (Brighton, Southern Publishing Company, 1894). 59pp., plans, tables, diagrs.

THOMSON, Dr. Theodore, *Report to the Local Government Board on an Epidemic of Enteric Fever in the Borough of Worthing.* . . (H.M.S.O., 1894). 31pp., tables.

PIKE, W. T. & Co., *A Descriptive Account of Worthing. Illustrated.* (Brighton, W. T. Pike, c.1895). 76pp., illus.

WORTHING GAZETTE COMPANY, *The Diamond Jubilee, 1897. Worthing Souvenir, Descriptive and Illustrative.* . . (Worthing, 1897). 64pp., illus.

SNEWIN, Edward, *Glimpses of Old Worthing as narrated by Edward Snewin and prepared for publication by an Old Inhabitant. Reprinted from the* Worthing Gazette *October 18th to December 20th 1899.* (Worthing, Gazette Company, 1900). 92pp., front.

SAYERS, Edward, *Transcripts of, and Extracts from, Records of the Past* [St. Andrews, West Tarring; St. Mary's Broadwater and Christ Church, Worthing] (W. J. C. Long, 1903). 183pp., illus.

CLUNN, Harold, 'Worthing: a historical sketch', in Clunn, H., *Famous South Coast Pleasure Resorts past and present* (T. Whittingham, 1929). pp. 347-362, illus.

FROST, Marian, *The early history of Worthing* (Hove, Combridges, 1929). 99pp., illus, bibliog.

AMBROSIANA: Letters and belongings of certain ladies of Ambrose Place, Worthing (Liverpool, July 1938). 194pp., front, illus (ports).

MIGEOD, F. W. H. editor, *Worthing: a survey of times past and present by local writers* . . . *on the occasion of the Forty-third Congress of the South Eastern Union of Scientific Societies to be held at Worthing, 21st to 25th June 1938* (Brighton and Worthing, 1938). 296pp., map.

ODELL, Mary T., *The Old Theatre, Worthing: The Theatre Royal 1807 to 1855* (Aylesbury, Geo. W. Jones, 1938). 163pp., illus.

SMAIL, Henfrey C. P., *The Worthing Road and its Coaches* (Worthing, 1943). 63pp., illus. (Worthing Pageant).

ODELL, Mary T., *More about the Old Theatre Worthing* (Worthing, 1945). 170pp., illus.

SNEWIN, Edward and SMAIL, Henfrey C. P., *Glimpses of Old Worthing* (Worthing, 1945). 170pp., illus. (Worthing Pageant)

LOOKER, Samuel J. editor, *Richard Jefferies: a tribute by various writers* (Worthing, 1946). 156pp., illus. (Worthing Cavalcade)

[GUTHRIE, James, and others], *Beach House* (Worthing, 1947). 64pp., illus.

LOOKER, Samuel J. editor, *William Henry Hudson: a tribute by various writers* (Worthing, 1947). 169pp., illus. (Worthing Cavalcade).

SMAIL, Henfrey C. P., *Coaching Times and after* (Worthing, 1948). 231pp., illus. (Worthing Pageant)

SMAIL, Henfrey C. P., *The Worthing Map story* (Worthing, 1949). 176pp., illus., maps. (Worthing Pageant)

LOOKER, Samuel J. editor, *Shelley, Trelawny and Henley. . .* (Worthing, 1950). 224pp., illus. (Worthing Cavalcade)

SMAIL, Henfrey C. P., *Offington, Broadwater Manor, Charmandean* (Worthing, 1950). 110pp., illus. (Worthing Pageant—Notable Houses of Worthing—2)

LONGLEY, A., *Down Our Way* (Worthing, *circa* 1951). 39pp., illus.

BROOKFIELD, H. C., 'Worthing: A Study of a modern coastal town', in *Town Planning Review*, Vol. 23 (1952), pp. 145-162.

SMAIL, Henfrey C. P., *Courtlands* (Worthing, 1952). 72pp., illus. (Worthing Pageant — Notable Houses of Worthing — 6)

SMAIL, Henfrey C. P., *Warwick House* (Worthing, 1952). 76pp., illus. (Worthing Pageant — Notable Houses of Worthing — 5)

LONGLEY, A., *Alexandra Terrace: introducing a Church, a Parish, a Terrace and some wanderings* (Worthing, E. G. Stead, 1960). 115pp., illus.

BICKERTON, Leonard M., F.L.A., F.M.A., *Worthing: a brief account of the history of the town from Neolithic times to the present day.* 3rd ed. (Worthing Museum, 1963.) 24pp., illus.

MARSHALL, R. A., *Worthing grown: a study of horticultural production under glass in Worthing and the West Sussex coast* (Worthing, R. A. Marshall, 1968). 40pp., illus., maps, tables, bibliog. Typescript thesis.

BRITISH TOURIST AUTHORITY, *A Report on visitors to Worthing, summer 1969* (BTA, 1970). 45pp., tables. Typescript.

HUXLEY-WILLIAMS, Muriel G., *A Brief Story of Heene in the County of Sussex: Domesday −1873−1973. To mark the occasion of the Centenary of St. Botolph's Church, Worthing* (Worthing, Rodney Press, 1973). 54pp., illus.

HARMER H. R. H., and ELLERAY, D. R., *A Picture of Worthing* (Chichester, West Sussex County Library Service, 1975). 32pp., illus.

HETZEL, Valerie, *A History of the William Davison Church of England High School for Girls Worthing, with particular reference to two outstanding personalities* (Brighton College of Education, 1975). 81pp., illus., maps, bibliog. Typescript thesis.